SOLID is not Solid

Five Object-Oriented Principles To Create a Codebase Everyone Will Hate

David Bryant Copeland

This book is copyright ©2019 by David Bryant Copeland, All Rights Reserved.

For more information, visit https://solid-is-not-solid.com

Contents

Contents

1 Stop Validating Your Experience and Start Questioning Authority — 1
  1.1 Literally Anyone Can Lead Thoughts — 2
  1.2 The Five Rules of Good Design That I'm Certain You Haven't Looked Closely At — 3
  1.3 SOLID is Not Very Solid After All — 3
  1.4 This is Not About Uncle Bob — 4

2 Single Responsibility Principle, or: Chasing Three Lines of Code Over 18 Files Just to Make One Change — 7
  2.1 What Exactly *is* a Responsibility? — 8
  2.2 Five Responsibilities in Five Lines of Code — 8
  2.3 Change, For Lack of a Better Word, is Good — 10
  2.4 The Second Stage Turbine Blade — 11
  2.5 Each Line of Code, Its Own Responsibility, Belongs Nestled Safely in its Own Class, Docker Container, or Microservice. — 12
  2.6 Incoherent Ramblings — 16
  2.7 Software Design Isn't About Counting Up Things — 20

3 Open/Closed Principle or: The Test Of Have You Actually Read SOLID — 23
  3.1 Inheritance — 24
  3.2 The Origin Story You Never Knew You Didn't Want — 27
  3.3 Version Numbers are For Marketing, Right? — 28

4 Liskov Substitution Principle or: Don't Use The One Thing Stroustrup Actually Didn't Want in C++ Anyway — 31
  4.1 Papers We Love But Have Not Really Read — 32
  4.2 Papers We Don't Love But Had To Read As Research For This Book — 32

5 Interface Segregation Principle or: The Reason Functional Programmers Are So Damn Smug   **35**
   5.1 Hacking Around Bad Design 35
   5.2 Ever Do Functional Programming in Java? 36
   5.3 Java Loves Interfaces So Much That It Does, In Fact, Marry Them 38

6 Dependency Inversion Principle, or: Why 2000s-era Java Code Was Mostly Written in XML   **41**
   6.1 Objects are All About Re-use. Just ask CORBA. . . I mean EJB 42
   6.2 I Will Make FizzBuzz Enterprise Edition Look Like Rails 45
   6.3 .java files are for Clean Coders Only 49

7 Agile's Infantilizing Sloganeering Diminishes Us All   **53**
   7.1 DRY - Don't Repeat Yourself. Do Not Repeat Yourself. Stop. Repeating. Yourself. 53
   7.2 KISS - I'm not Stupid, and Neither Are You 55
   7.3 YAGNI - You Aren't Gonna Need It (except when you are) 56
   7.4 The Simplest Thing That Could Possibly Work Would Be Actually Working Software 56
   7.5 No Big Design Up Front So Why Aren't You Coding Right Now? Start Coding. Now. Just Type "v" "i" "m". 57
   7.6 User Stories Paint a Picture of Fairy Tales and Form Validations 58

8 Well, *Now* What Do We Do?   **61**
   8.1 Some Solid Advice 61
   8.2 Some Words of Warning 62
   8.3 Not Convinced? 62

9 Colophon or: How To Make Your Own e-Book!   **63**

1
Stop Validating Your Experience and Start Questioning Authority

Reading books and attending talks where your experience, opinions, and beliefs are validated is pretty powerful. Validation can be a wonderful thing, as it can let you know that you are not alone in how you feel. Like when you saw a sixteen-level indented series of callbacks on the NodeJS home page and thought maybe, just maybe, this was not the future of web development.

But it can also blind you to the truth. By default, you are misinformed (everyone is). If all you are exposed to is information re-affirming that misinformed thinking, you'll miss out on a lot. You might stop critically thinking about what you are told. And if you don't get any sort of feedback, you won't even realize it.

Building and maintaining software is difficult, primarily because there is no feedback available for how well you've done your job. Working in software always feels painful, slow, and annoying (even when it's not really that bad). What this means is that it's really hard to know if the advice you've been given about how to do it actually worked.

And programming is such a unique experience that there really is no analogy for it that we can look to for guidance. It's not engineering, it's not a craft, it's not science, and it's definitely not art.[1] But it's damn fun!

---

[1] OK, well, **Haskell** is an art project.

One thing that's great about programming is that it has a pretty low barrier to entry. Anyone who has access to a computer can learn to program. Despite that, the field has always been rife with gatekeepers who try to describe what *real* programming is. But, those gates slowly are coming down and it turns out that lots of people are good at programming. Even computer science majors. This has a downside, though.

That downside is opinions, hot takes, thought leaders, conference speakers, and book authors[2] all giving their opinions about their experience and trying to generalize those into rules about how to be a good programmer... all without any real evidence other than survivorship bias.

1.1 Literally Anyone Can Lead Thoughts

Do you know what I had to do to write and publish this? The hardest part was figuring out how to change fonts in LaTeX[3]. 20 years ago the hardest part would've been to find a publisher and decide to be OK with a 10% royalty rate. Today, I don't need anyone's permission to make a *book*. On paper!

It turns out that almost everything you've been told about how to design software went through the same vetting process (by which I mean learning LaTeX).

What this should tell you is that everything you were told was someone trying to convey their experience in a way that made sense and that validates their worldview. This is not bad or evil, but it is also why science exists. Science is less susceptible to biases like survivorship bias. But software development is not based on science. At all.[4]

---

[2] Hi.

[3] LaTeX is a typesetting system that produces beautiful output, but is so arcane, it makes stored procedures look like Elixir. Debugging it makes you pine for an error message as straightforward as "undefined is not a function". That said, there's really nothing better after all this time.

[4] It's actually illuminating when you come to understand and accept that almost everything you hold dear about programming has no scientific basis for being useful. Pairing, TDD, MVC, Rails, Style Guides, Cucumber, and Functional Programming have never been evaluated as to their fitness to produce good software in any real way. Vim is the only thing proven to make you awesome. I can't find the paper right now but I'm *positive* vim has been double-blind control-trialed many, many times. Trust me.

So this brings us to SOLID[5].

1.2 The Five Rules of Good Design That I'm Certain You Haven't Looked Closely At

We are told that the SOLID Principles are the cornerstone of good object-oriented design. But they were developed, in part, as defense mechanisms against the lack of object-oriented features in C++ and Java. If Smalltalk had won the language wars, there would be no SOLID.[6]

When I see Ruby programmers invoke the Single Responsibility Principle, thus sending them and their team into a tailspin of debating what exactly *is* a responsibility, I can't help wondering if there's actually *not* something to SOLID after all.

Maybe it was just a way for Robert Martin to fight the last war, vent a bit of frustration, and try to impart the wisdom of his experience onto others, even if his problems aren't our problems, and the context in which his experience makes sense isn't one we find ourselves in these days.

So I had a look.

And I can't say I was enlightened by what I found. I guess it *did* make me realize that the Open/Closed Principle is Dada-level nonsense, but very little of what I read seemed practically useful. Having seen engineers apply these principles to disastrous effects, I'm left wanting. Why the heck do we talk about these principles at all?

So let's tear them down.

1.3 SOLID is Not Very Solid After All

Let's see what is going on with these principles and try to figure out what they are teaching us. But let's also keep in mind that they are not presented as guidelines, patterns, or suggestions, but as *principles*. A principle is:

---

[5] https://en.wikipedia.org/wiki/SOLID

[6] Though let's be honest, there would instead be MUSH: Malleable, Unmaintainable, Slow, and Heavy software. All respect to Smalltalk, but that was just never gonna work out.

> a fundamental truth or proposition that serves as the foundation for a system of belief or behavior or for a chain of reasoning.

Fundamental truths, these are not. Pretty much *all* they say is this:

- **Single Responsibility Principle**: don't write too much code in one place, in fact just make single method classes that have only one line of code in them.
- **Open/Closed Principle**: make code so flexible you don't have to write it, because you aren't allowed to change it anyway.
- **Liskov Substitution Principle**: don't base logic on run-time types and also there is a CS paper that is not really related to this written by a Turing Award Winner! Legit!
- **Interface Segregation Principle**: use Java interfaces to mask the bloated API of your classes.
- **Dependency Inversion Principle**: write all your code in XML configuration files.

There's actually *not much* on offer from the SOLID principles when you dig into them, as I have done. But there's a lot of harm due to how they are written and the vague language they use.

Let me put it this way: I've seen programmers create some horrible abominations in my day (including myself). SOLID didn't help steer us in the right direction. Usually, it made things worse.[7]

So join me for this snarky take that *does* include a vein of truth and quite possibly can teach you something about how to *think* about design. But first, a word about the progenitor of all this: Robert "Uncle Bob" Martin.

1.4 This is Not About Uncle Bob

I have been inspired by Uncle Bob[8], mostly by his writing and conference talks. There was a brief time that I appealed to his au-

---

[7]Yes, I just told you to believe something based on my lived experience. But, I'm hanging a lantern on it right here in this footnote.

[8]I'll be referring to Robert Martin as Uncle Bob because that's how I first came to know of him and it's a bit more amusing to refer to him that way.

thority, since so much of what he had written about had validated my own experience. And there's a core to Uncle Bob's message over the years that *is good*. He clearly cares very deeply about writing good software and helping others to do the same.

And because of this, along with his major impact on object-oriented programming, his ideas are not only *worth* criticizing, but I think they *must* be criticized and examined. Someone in power must have their ideas challenged or things get bad. Heck, I dream of the day someone learns enough LaTeX to criticize *my* work!

But that's all I'm aiming to do: criticize ideas.[9] I don't know Uncle Bob at all and I assume that all of his work over the years comes from a place of good intentions. But even if it doesn't, it doesn't matter. This is about some of his ideas and how they are interpreted, not about him.

So, without further ado, let's dig into the Single Responsibility Principle, also known as the Why Did You Deign To Write More Than One Line of Code In A Method Principle.

---

[9]This isn't *all* Uncle Bob. Some of his contemporaries get some drive-bys after I take down SOLID, because shit like YAGNI and KISS is a bit problematic. I also promise that if this book sells well, the follow up, "XP: The Way to Motivate Little Children To Close JIRA Tickets At A Big Horrible Technology Company Run By People Who Do Not Understand Technology", will be dedicated to Kent Beck. He's given us some real doozies over the years.

2

Single Responsibility Principle, or: Chasing Three Lines of Code Over 18 Files Just to Make One Change

It's fitting we start with Single Responsibility Principle, because it's by far the most insidious of the SOLID principles. The reason is that if you do what it says, you end up with horribly complex code that requires hiking all over Hell's Half Acre to understand. Yet the principle certainly *sounds* legit, so we follow it as best we can (usually to the ends of the Earth).

So what is the Single Responsibility Principle? There's a few definitions, so let's start with Wikipedia's[1]:

---

[1] https://en.wikipedia.org/wiki/Single_responsibility_principle

> A class should only have a single responsibility, that is, only changes to one of the software's specifications should be able to affect the specification of the class

Raise your hand if you've built a piece of software from a *specification*. No? Yeah, me neither. I appreciate the attempt at formality but as mentioned earlier, computer science this is not. So, let's just assume the tuxedo that's hung on this definition isn't as pressed as we think.

The key here is "responsibility". What does that mean?

2.1 What Exactly *is* a Responsibility?

Rather than head to the dictionary, let's keep digging and see how Uncle Bob defines responsibility. He's quoted as saying:

> a responsibility is a *reason to change*

I can think of at least two reasons a class might need to change: fixing bugs and adding features.[2]

I'm sure Uncle Bob has both fixed bugs and added features, so this can't be what he means. And yet we don't have much else to go on.

Here's why this principle is so troubling. There *is* a kernel of truth to it. We really don't want our classes doing too much stuff. But why? And why is "two responsibilities" too much? And what's stopping us from redefining a class' responsibility such that it only has a single one? We don't have a lot of clarity here.

Let's look at some code.

2.2 Five Responsibilities in Five Lines of Code

On the first day of Ruby on Rails school, you learn about `rails new`, but on the *second* day, you make a controller to save an Active Record into the database based on someone having filled out

---

[2] Three, if you've installed Rubocop and committed the grave sin of misplacing a comma.

a web form. This controller will indicate which form fields are allowed, it will validate the values, and then either save the record or re-render the form to show the user what they screwed up.

We'll use the extremely common domain that everyone is familiar with instinctively, which is managing a database of professional wrestlers.[3]

Here's a controller for saving a new wrestler:

```ruby
class WrestlersController
  def create
    @wrestler = Wrestler.create(wrestler_params)
    if @wrestler.valid?
      redirect_to wrestlers_path
    else
      render :new
    end
  end

  private

  def wrestler_params
    params.require(:wrestler).permit(
      :name, :hails_from, :finishing_move, :weight)
  end
end
```

If you look up "vanilla" in the dictionary, you will find this controller method. It's exactly how Rails wants you to work and it's a pretty focused routine.

Does it violate the Single Responsibility Principle? The answer depends on how we define "responsibility". If we say that the responsibility of this controller is to manage the workflow of making new wrestlers, then this controller passes with flying colors!

But, we could also say that this controller validates parameters, interacts with the database, and handles user view rendering.

---

[3]I'm almost certain that top wrestling leagues use software like this to keep track of their roster. You can be sure if your local promotion is struggling, it's absolutely due to a lack of software. I mean, what problem *isn't* due to a lack of software, amirite?

That is three responsibilities which, to be very explicit, is more than one. A violation!

This is the problem with these "principles". They tell you what to do with no nuance, no context, and no freaking backstory. What problem are we even trying to solve by counting responsibilities?

The problem we are solving is that we want our code to be easy to change when we get new requirements.

2.3 Change, For Lack of a Better Word, is Good

What sort of changes might we get asked to make related to creating wrestlers? Well, we could be asked to store their real name, or we could be asked to route users to the new wrestler's page instead of the index page after successful creation, or we could be asked to send an email to HHH[4] any time one gets created.

While these are three reasons to change our controller code, would these changes actually change the responsibility of the code? Who knows?

Let's just make one of these changes and see what happens. Let's send an email to the front office whenever a new wrestler is successfully created. In Rails, sending an email is just one line of code[5], so we'll add it right before we do the redirect:

```
class WrestlersController
  def create
    @wrestler = Wrestler.create(wrestler_params)
    if @wrestler.valid?
→     FrontOfficeMailer.new_wrestler(@wrestler).
→       deliver_now!
      redirect_to :index
    else
      render :new
    end
  end

  private
```

---
[4]https://en.wikipedia.org/wiki/Triple_H
[5]Probably why Rails doesn't scale.

```
    def wrestler_params
      params.require(:wrestler).permit(
          :name, :hails_from, :finishing_move, :weight)
    end
end
```

Have we violated Single Responsibility Principle *now*? Or did we violate it *harder* than before?

Let me propose another way to think about code. Instead of "reasons to change", "responsibilities", or "specifications", let's talk about *cohesion*.

2.4 The Second Stage Turbine Blade

Cohesion is a vague term, but it's commonly used when discussing the design of software. Wikipedia has a definition that works[6].

> Cohesion refers to the degree to which the elements inside a module belong together. In one sense, it is a measure of the strength of relationship between the methods and data of a class and some unifying purpose or concept served by that class. In another sense, it is a measure of the strength of relationship between the class's methods and data themselves.

Now, this isn't as quantifiable as counting up responsibilities and determining that if we have counted more than one, we must hang our heads in shame for the crime of trying to write too much code at once, but it *does* give us some more concrete clues as to *how to think about the design of our code.*

This is a *huge* problem with a lot of the agile dogma and object-oriented design advice. It is not described in a way to help you learn how to *think* about problems. Instead, we get a lot of context-free commandments and cute aphorisms that we can't apply to unknown situations without bringing in highly-paid consultants.[7]

---

[6]https://en.wikipedia.org/wiki/Cohesion_(computer_science)
[7]Oh wait, did I say that out loud?

The clue is the phrase "strength of the relationship between the methods and data of a class and some unifying purpose or concept". *This* is what we're aiming at.

A cohesive class is one in which its contents are unified around some concept. *Maybe* we could call this a "responsibility", but I like to use words in the right way, since words have, you know, meaning and stuff.

"Responsibility" is just not the right word for what we are talking about here (neither is "reason to change"). In fact, any code review where the Single Responsibility Principle is invoked makes this problem plainly clear, because the developers stop talking about the code and start talking what a responsibility actually is.

It's not surprising that the consultants who signed the Agile Manifesto might not have actually run across this problem. The power dynamics in play whenever an *expert* is brought in make it hard to have a real discussion. I mean, who better to tell us what is and is not a responsibility than the guy that coined the principle, right? But it doesn't change the fact that if you smooth out the power dynamics, yelling slogans and proclaiming the answers by fiat just doesn't work. You actually have to discuss the code itself!

Anyway, why is it bad if our code isn't cohesive?

It depends on *how* it's not cohesive, and there are two ways this happens. Code can either lack cohesion, in which case a single concept is spread out all over the place, or it can be incoherent, where a single blob of code ensconces multiple intermingled concepts.

It's the second problem that the Single Responsibility Principle wants to solve, but it usually does it by aggressive decoupling, thus creating the first problem.

2.5 Each Line of Code, Its Own Responsibility, Belongs Nestled Safely in its Own Class, Docker Container, or Microservice.

Since all of this nonsense is to make our code easier to change, let us refactor our original controller to comply with the Single Responsibility Principle, and then see how easy it is to change.

So look, ye, upon our Rails controller, and know that it is bad, for it has *too many* responsibilities, since it validates parameters, writes to the database, and yet also routes users to a view based on the validity of their form submission.

Let us now separate these woefully disparate concerns so that our code might become *maintainable*.

First, we'll extract that pesky routing logic into a `WrestlerRouter` class.

```ruby
class WrestlerRouter
  def new_wrestler(controller, wrestler)
    if wrestler.valid?
      controller.redirect_to :index
    else
      controller.render :new
    end
  end
end
```

We'll then remove all that nasty code about actually creating a wrestler from parameters into a `WrestlerCreator` class.

```ruby
class WrestlerCreator
  def create(params)
    Wrestler.create(wrestler_params(params))
  end

private

  def wrestler_params(params)
    params.require(:wrestler).permit(
      :name, :hails_from, :finishing_move, :weight)
  end
end
```

Armed with these two classes that each have *only one reason to change*, we can recreate our `WrestlersController`.

```
class WrestlersController
  def create
    @wrestler = WrestlerCreator.new.create(params)
    WrestlerRouter.new.new_wrestler(self,@wrestler)
  end
end
```

What evil is this?

Where is the concept of wrestler creation now? It is in three classes (in three different files). To get an understanding of the concept of wrestler creation *as it is currently defined* requires looking in three different places. This code lacks cohesion. It's as if its subatomic structure has been severed, left floating in the void of space.

What this means is that, when we have to change something about wrestler creation, we have to look in all three classes and *hope* that our change fits into one of the extracted structures we've created.

Let's now implement our front-office emailing requirement. Remember, we want to send an email only if we saved a valid wrestler to the database. Where would that go in this structure?

We could put it in the `WrestlerRouter`, because that's where we check for validity, but it seems *pretty weird* for a router to be sending email.

I know, we'll use *callbacks*!

Let's flexibilize the `WrestlerRouter` so that we can pass in some arbitrary code to execute whenever a valid wrestler has been identified.

```
    class WrestlerRouter
      def new_wrestler(controller, wrestler, on_valid=nil)
        if wrestler.valid?
→         unless on_valid.nil?
→           on_valid.(wrestler)
→         end
          controller.redirect_to :index
        else
          controller.render :new
        end
```

```
        end
    end
```

Our class is so much more flexible (incidentally making it compliant with some other SOLID principles).

To use this feature, we'll make a lambda that sends email and pass that lambda in to `new_wrestler`.

```
    class WrestlersController
      def create
→       on_valid = ->(wrestler) {
→         FrontOfficeMailer.new_wrestler(wrestler).
→           deliver_now!
→       }
        @wrestler = WrestlerCreator.new.create(params)
→       WrestlerRouter.new.
→         new_wrestler(self, @wrestler, on_valid)
      end
    end
```

I bet you didn't think we could make the code worse, did you? This is just...eck. Instead of a design where a simple change required the addition of single line of code, we adhered to the Single Responsibility Principle and created a situation in which a simple change required changing the public API of a class (which you'll discover in the next chapter is not allowed), and then adding several lines of code overall.

The reason is not because we miscounted responsibilities. It's because our design of a "bunch of small single purpose classes" lacked cohesion. None of the classes we created represents a full concept, based on the current definition of those concepts. Creating a wrestler is not complex, so why did we make it that way?

We did it because Uncle Bob says we must have only one reason to change, but he did not define what a reason is, so we made a very reasonable assumption and created a set of pure nonsense that junior developers will copy and senior developers will curse and all because we did what some principle said because principles are there for us to follow and not guidelines which would invite thinking through nor are they design patterns which are usually clear about when and how they should be applied so that we can make sure we are balancing all the right tradeoffs and not just appealing to authority.

We could've prevented this with two simple questions:

- Does the method implement a complete concept? If yes, don't touch it.
- Does the proposed change affect cohesion? If not, the change is fine as it is.

In our case, the original code was short and cohesive; it implemented the entirety of wrestler creation. The change to send an email didn't affect its cohesion, so we should've just done that.

Granted, cohesiveness is hard to quantify as it requires alignment across the team about what a concept is. Keep in mind that "concept" here really is a "domain concept". If the team isn't aligned around *that*, you have much bigger problems.

But why would Uncle Bob create this principle? He's not stupid and has a ton of experience that we can't just ignore. He wouldn't just make up nonsense.[8]

Imagine that we continue development and keep getting new requirements over a long period of time. We address them one line at a time, as we did with the first new requirement. Even if that code is all part of wrestler creation conceptually, there's a point at which there is just too much code.

Would *this* be when to count responsibilities?

No. We can still use cohesion to get a clearer understanding.

2.6 Incoherent Ramblings

Let us fast-forward to a world where we've added the following requirements to creating a wrestler:

---

[8]The Open/Closed Principle notwithstanding.

- The front office must be notified on all new wrestlers...
- except if that wrestler is from Canada. In that case we notify our Canadian office...
- unless that wrestler is under 200 pounds (14.3 stone). In *this* case we notify the cruiserweight division...
- unless that wrestler has no finishing move. In this case we notify the developmental territory.

We got these requirements at different times and each only required a couple lines of code to implement. Adding those one or two lines is a reasonable approach. Doing so results in this:

```ruby
class WrestlersController
  def create
    @wrestler = Wrestler.create(wrestler_params)
    if @wrestler.valid?
      if @wrestler.finishing_move.blank?
        DevelopmentalMailer.new_wrestler(@wrestler).
          deliver_now!
      elsif @wrestler.weight < 200
        CruiserweightMailer.new_wrestler(@wrestler).
          deliver_now!
      elsif @wrestler.hails_from =~ /canada/i
        CanadianOffice.new_wrestler(@wrestler).
          deliver_now!
      else
        FrontOfficeMailer.new_wrestler(@wrestler).
          deliver_now!
      end
      redirect_to wrestlers_path
    else
      render :new
    end
  end

private

  def wrestler_params
    params.require(:wrestler).permit(
      :name, :hails_from, :finishing_move, :weight)
```

```
      end
end
```

Wow, it's not looking so good, but it's still all unified around this concept of creating wrestlers. So it's cohesive, but it's also complex. What do we do?

Cohesion is about concepts and they can be fractal. We can now pretty clearly see that the concept of emailing someone about new wrestlers has gotten complex. It stands on its own.

We shouldn't change it now just because it looks gross, but if we get another requirement around sending emails, that might be a time to think about changing things.

So let's suppose we get such a change. The developmental territory needs to know about wrestlers that hail from "Parts Unknown", because even for professional wrestling that is a bit of a stretch.

Knowing that our controller method is incoherent (multiple fleshed-out concepts are intermingled), and with the need to go into the code and change it, now is a good time to refactor. We just have to do it such that the resulting code is cohesive. The thing we want to avoid is decoupling so much that we lose all cohesion.

You might be thinking we should've done this earlier. You might even think if we had done it from the start we wouldn't be in this pickle. But we didn't know how many of these changes were coming down the pike, so we did the best with what we knew at the time. Maybe the fourth requirement should've triggered the refactor we're about to make. I like to look for patterns on the *third* such data point, but you do you. Just remember that one data point doesn't represent a trend.

Let's extract all that email logic into a `NewWrestlerEmailer`:

```
class NewWrestlerEmailer
  def new_wrestler(wrestler)
    if wrestler.finishing_move.blank?
      DevelopmentalMailer.new_wrestler(wrestler).
        deliver_now!
```

```ruby
      elsif wrestler.weight < 200
        CruiserweightMailer.new_wrestler(wrestler).
          deliver_now!
      elsif wrestler.hails_from =~ /canada/i
        CanadianOffice.new_wrestler(wrestler).
          deliver_now!
      else
        FrontOfficeMailer.new_wrestler(wrestler).
          deliver_now!
      end
    end
  end
```

We can then replace all this code in `WrestlersController`:

```ruby
  class WrestlersController
    def create
      @wrestler = Wrestler.create(wrestler_params)
      if @wrestler.valid?
→       NewWrestlerEmailer.new.new_wrestler(@wrestler)
        redirect_to wrestlers_path
      else
        render :new
      end
    end

  private

    def wrestler_params
      params.require(:wrestler).permit(
        :name, :hails_from,:finishing_move, :weight)
    end
  end
```

With this refactor, we have the same size of change to account for wrestlers hailing from parts unknown, but we now have a nice cohesive piece of code that has the email logic...and nothing else[9].

These two classes don't lack cohesion, as they represent two well-defined concepts on our domain: creating wrestlers and emailing someone when they got created. And neither class is incoherent, since they only have code about their respective concepts.

So did we just create the "Single Concept Principle"? And isn't all this what the Single Responsibility Principle was trying to tell us?

2.7 Software Design Isn't About Counting Up Things

Maybe this is all what Uncle Bob intended, but it really isn't written that way, nor is it discussed this way, nor do people apply the principle in the way we just did. Words have meaning and "responsibility" is not the right word. Even "concept" is a bit fluid, so if we called this the "Single Concept Principle", the engineers would argue about "concept".

The thing is, software design isn't about counting up things and deciding the design is good or bad. Our code can, and should, be evaluated for cohesion, and this is a necessarily fuzzy concept.

If you think your code is cohesive, don't mess with it! If it's not, refactor it so that it is. But when discussing what to do, stay close to the code and the problem it solves. Avoid making a decision by counting things.

When you think about cohesion, understand that this is rooted in the *concepts of your business domain* and not about the code. Code can't be cohesive just on its own. It has to have the context of the domain. And when that context changes, the code might suddenly lose cohesion!

I know I promised you a short book, and we just spent 14 pages on the first SOLID principle. I promise the remainder aren't this long,

---

[9] I bet those if statements offend your sensibilities. They are pretty gross, but they are also pretty straightforward, and you know they work. You Java developers are probably cool right now, but you Rubyists, I just *know* you want to meta-program those if statements away. Admit it. I feel it, too. Resist. if statements are nice if you just get to know them.

mostly because they are harder to understand and more useless. In my experience, the Single Responsibility Principle is the only SOLID principle anyone bothers with, and after everyone's argued out about what is and is not a responsibility, there's no time left for anything else.

3

Open/Closed Principle or: The Test Of Have You Actually Read SOLID

The Open/Closed Principle tells us—directly and in no uncertain terms—that you cannot change source code.

You think I'm kidding? The principle states that classes[1] should be "open for extension, but closed for modification." Here's how Uncle Bob defines a class that is "closed for modification"[2]:

> The source code of such a [class] is inviolate.[3] No one is allowed to make source code changes to it.

No one. Is **allowed**. So... we're just supposed to write it all perfectly the first time? How?

You want to know the truth about the solution or have you always known? You've just hidden it away. You know the truth. Say it.

---

[1] Remember, this is a *principle* so the implication is not *some* classes, but *all* classes.

[2] https://web.archive.org/web/20060822033314/http://www.objectmentor.com/resources/articles/ocp.pdf

[3] According to the dictionary this word means "free or safe from injury or violation", which is pretty strange way to talk about *source code*. One wonders where Uncle Bob got his thesaurus from.

3.1 Inheritance

According to the principle, "abstraction is key" in dealing with classes whose source code **no one is allowed to change**. We must create a class that has all the necessary extension points so that we can use inheritance to override its behavior, and *then* we must never ever use the class directly, but instead rely on an abstract base class.

Let's see an example. Suppose we need to know which wrestlers are hard workers and which aren't. We can do that by averaging up the length of their matches. Anyone who averages more than 20 minutes is a hard worker.

We'll use a generic class called `Averager` to abstract the logic of calculating an average.

```
class Averager
  def average(list_of_numbers)
    total = 0
    list_of_numbers.each do |number|
      total += number
    end
    total / list_of_numbers.size
  end
end

class Wrestler
  def hard_worker?
    average_match_length = Averager.new.average(
        self.matches.map(&:length))

    average_match_length > 20
  end
end
```

This is a clear violation of the open/closed principle, because what if we want to store our running total some other way? What if we want to use a banker's rounding for division? What if we just signed a platinum-level partnership agreement with a hot new startup call Addr that just got $40,000,000 in a Series A for their addition-as-a-service startup and it was from the same venture capitalist that provided us our seed round and now we have to integrate with them so that Addr can put our logo onto their homepage and make the board think they are doing a good job at enterprise sales?

Think of the horror of having to modify this source code!

Fortunately, we can apply the Open/Closed Principle to fix this egregious design mistake.

First, we'll need an `AbstractAverager` that has all the flexibility we could ever need. Ruby doesn't have abstract methods, but I've added them as documentation so future SOLID developers know how to extend things (I'm not a monster).

```ruby
class AbstractAverager
  def average(list_of_numbers)
    initialize_total
    iterate_over_list(list_of_numbers) do |element|
      add_element_to_running_total(element)
    end
    compute_average(list_of_numbers.size)
  end

  def initialize_total
    raise "Implement this to initialize your total counter"
  end

  def iterate_over_list(list_of_numbers)
    raise "Implement this to yield each number. " +
          "_each_ number. Get it?"
  end

  def add_element_to_running_total(element)
    raise "Hey, I like +, but maybe you like +=. " +
          "Or maybe you like tight loops and bit " +
          "shifting.  We push up a big tent here."
  end

  def compute_average(list_size)
    raise "Don't let those pesky data scientists " +
```

```
          "tell YOU how to average numbers.  This " +
          "is DEEP LEARNING here!"
    end
end
```

With this clean abstraction, we can now create the dirty concrete implementation that hopefully we won't have to touch once we've written it.

```
class FilthyUnchangeableConcreteAverager < AbstractAverager
  def initialize_total
    @total = 0
  end

  def total
    @total
  end

  def iterate_over_list(list)
    list.each do |element|
      yield element
    end
  end

  def add_element_to_running_total(element)
    update_total(total + element)
  end

  def update_total(new_total)
    @total = new_total
  end

  def compute_average(size_of_list)
    total / size_of_list
  end
end

class Wrestler
  def hard_worker?(averager)
    average_match_length = averager.average(
```

```
      self.matches.map(&:length))

    average_match_length > 20
  end
end
```

Whew! Now our class is open for modification, so we can freely "make the module behave in new and different ways as the requirements of the application change or to meet the needs of new applications."

Ridiculous? Sure. But more ridiculous than saying you cannot change the source code?

Where in Leto's name did this principle even come from?!?!?

3.2 The Origin Story You Never Knew You Didn't Want

The origin of the Open/Closed Principle came from Uncle Bob over-reaching on an observation Bertrand Meyer made in his book Object-Oriented Software Construction[4].

In that book, Meyer talks about managing API versioning, arguing that, while we want to be able to add new features and change code, that can create a problem if we make a breaking change (in Meyer's case, it was related to pre-compiled binaries dynamically linking to changed code and the binary incompatibilities this would create).

This is a real problem! But making overly flexible classes, abstract base classes, and using inheritance is not the way to solve it. OK, it's *a* way but it's certainly not the *only* way.

Meyer's book was written in the 80s. At that time, things were different. As the final notes of "Hold Back The Rain" played from side one of Duran Duran's "Rio", most programmers would initiate the compilation step of their shared library, walk over to the record player, flip the record, and carefully drop the needle *right* at the start of "Save a Prayer", hoping not to hear any part of "Last

---

[4]https://www.amazon.com/Object-Oriented-Software-Construction-Book-CD-ROM/dp/0136291554/ref=sr_1_1

Chance on a Stairway" but also hoping their C library would now be built and ready to be copied to a CD-ROM for distribution.[5]

Having to repeat this cycle was expensive, so it makes sense to try to think through ways to deal with the need to extend code that you had stamped into a spinning rusted metal disk four states away without having to recompile and redistribute the entire thing.

Nowadays, this isn't quite the problem it was then. Your average JavaScript project can literally use every single version of the `isarray` module[6] *at the same time* and there's no problem[7].

To make a long story short, Meyer was trying to find a way to manage versioning of shared libraries in a compiled pre-Internet world in which his product was code libraries that people paid for and installed on disks manually. That is not a problem we have today. Did you know that some languages aren't even *compiled* anymore?

3.3 Version Numbers are For Marketing, Right?

API versioning *is* a problem, but there are a lot of ways to handle that other than inheritance. As it turns out, the best way to handle the need to make breaking changes is "make everyone change their code to use the latest version."

Nevertheless, Uncle Bob decided that all of our classes must be built as highly-extensible abstract classes and that no class should explicitly depend on any actual implementation, all so we could not have to change the source code in order to get new and different behavior.

Given this backstory, and the utterly nonsensical way in which the Open/Closed Principle is stated, I now believe that this principle is instead a test to see just how much bullshit one is willing to put up with before questioning what authority figures say.

---

[5] It usually took longer, which is why so many programmers are into prog-rock.
[6] https://www.npmjs.com/package/isarray
[7] Well, except for the introduction of a *massive* attack surface and a bloated download, but I read somewhere that network bandwidth is infinite (at least in Menlo Park), so the way Node does package management is fine. Totally fine.

So yes, consider versioning issues when making changes. Consider who is using your code and by all means *try* to make backwards compatible changes. But don't add in tons of flexibility the first time just because you might need to change stuff later. You aren't gonna need it.

4

Liskov Substitution Principle or: Don't Use The One Thing Stroustrup Actually Didn't Want in C++ Anyway

I'm starting to think Uncle Bob likes inheritance. The Liskov Substitution Principle takes a computer science paper about subtyping, and, over 11 pages, tells us not to look at the type of objects at run-time or bad things will happen.

I'm inclined to just stop here, because in what world is this *such* a problem that it needs a *principle* to help us avoid?

That said, I do need to bail out Barbara Liskov, whose name got attached to this principle. Unlike us programmers, Barbara Liskov is a legit computer scientist. She does real research, writes real papers, and won the Turing Award! We owe it to her to explain how her name got on this, because she did *not* win the Turing Award for this principle.

4.1 Papers We Love But Have Not Really Read

Barbara Liskov and Jeannette Wing authored a paper[1] that explores the definition of *subtypes* as it related to program correctness. They state that if an object y has all the properties of object x, then we can safely use y anywhere we use x and that y is a subtype of x. If y does *not* have all the properties of x, it is not a subtype of x.

Neat.

Most programming languages implement a somewhat... looser definition of subtyping. Java, for example, allows any object y to be used in place of any object x so long as y's class inherits (directly or transitively) from x's, *or* if x and y implement the same interface. In Ruby, pass whatever to whatever, it's cool, don't worry about it, we have duck typing and if it quacks like a monkey with a duck taped to its stomach then everything will work fine until Rails 6.2 which deprecates taping, but you can install the rails-duck-taping gem to get that feature back.

So what does this have to do with object-oriented design? Not much.

4.2 Papers We Don't Love But Had To Read As Research For This Book

Uncle Bob read Liskov and Wing's paper, forgot about Wing, and then wrote 11 pages that boil down to "do not base logic on the run time type of an object".

This is good advice! Let's see why.

We need to model wrestling events. There will be a base event and then classes for the actual events can extend that. There is a house show (non-televised event), a TV taping, and a pay-per-view, which is like a TV taping, but about four hours longer.

```
class WrestlingEvent
  # ...
end
```

---

[1] http://reports-archive.adm.cs.cmu.edu/anon/1999/CMU-CS-99-156.ps

```ruby
class HouseShow < WrestlingEvent
end

class TVTaping < WrestlingEvent
end

class PPV < TVTaping
end
```

Perfect. The problem arises when we automate spamming social media about these events, because we need to use a different mechanism based on the type of event.

```ruby
def spam_social_media(events)
  events.each do |event|
    if event.kind_of?(HouseShow)
      influencers.each do |influencer|
        authentically_post_to_the_gram(influencer,event)
      end
    elsif event.kind_of?(TVTaping)
      ask_russia_to_put_it_on_facebook(event)
    elseif event.kind_of?(PPV)
      local_sportsball_games.each do |game|
        run_tv_ad(game, event)
      end
    end
  end
end
```

If we introduce a new type of event, `WeAreOKWithTakingSaudiMoneyEvent`, our `spam_social_media` routine doesn't work right.

This is a real problem and is one example of why you should not base logic on the run time type of an object. Does this need to be a principle of object-oriented design? I don't know. But if it *did*, why would Uncle Bob state it[2] this way:

---
[2]https://web.archive.org/web/20150905081111/http://www.objectmentor.com/resources/articles/lsp.pdf

> Functions that use pointers or references to base classes must be able to use objects of derived classes without knowing it.

Pointers? References? It's like 1996, and we're all doing the Macarena again[3]. It also doesn't say anything about the actual problem outlined in the 11-page paper. Why can't these goddamn principles just come out and say what they mean? Ugh.

The paper, after outlining the problems with basing logic on run-time types, goes seriously off the rails with a convoluted example using a `Square` class that extends `Rectangle` and in the end there is no actual advice on what problem we were solving or what to do.

While the Open/Closed Principle was a test of how well one questions authority in the face of utter nonsense, *this* principle exists to provide the "L" needed to make the SOLID acronym work. Poor Wing never had a chance.

---

[3]Yes, I know that Go has these things and it's modern language. I like to think of it as a modernist language, embodying concepts last in vogue during the early 20th century. I mean, write yourself a microservice in Go and tell me how modern you feel. While you are at it, try changing a few random & to * and watch as your app still compiles but then panics at run-time. So, so modern.

5
Interface Segregation Principle or: The Reason Functional Programmers Are So Damn Smug

The Interface Segregation Principle states that "no client should be forced to depend on a method it does not use". Do we get a definition of "forced" or "depend"? No we don't.

Much like the Single Responsibility Principle, the draconian absolutist wording of this only creates problems. Fortunately, it only creates problems in a static language like Java or Scala. If you have to work in those languages, you have much bigger problems than SOLID.[1]

For completeness though, let's see what the hubbub is about.

5.1 Hacking Around Bad Design

Uncle Bob's paper[2] summarizes the problem like so:

---

[1] Can you *believe* Java was created for whatever the hell a "set top box" was in the 90's? And *this* is what powers the Walden Books competitor where we run our virtual servers? What a time to be alive.

[2] https://drive.google.com/file/d/0BwhCYaYDn8EgOTViYjJhYzMtMzYxMC0 0MzFjLWJjMzYtOGJiMDc5N2JkYmJi/view

> The ISP acknowledges that there are objects that require non-cohesive interfaces; however it suggests that clients should not know about them as a single class. Instead, clients should know about abstract base classes that have cohesive interfaces. Some languages refer to these abstract base classes as "interfaces", "protocols" or "signatures".

What this is saying is that if, for some reason, we need to have a class defined with a ton of methods that are not cohesive (which would be impossible since we are following the Single Responsibility Principle!), and that users of this class only need to use *some* of those methods, we should create interfaces or abstract base classes with only those methods being used so that users can depend on these cohesive interfaces.

Sure, maybe. But also maybe don't make a non-cohesive class in the first place? And what is the exact problem caused by having everyone depend on this non-cohesive class? Unclear and unstated.

I will now show you where this principle leads and it's nowhere good. Remember, I have read the backstory of this principle and came up empty. This means I know enough to ignore it, but I guarantee most developers haven't done that, and will follow the principle as stated.

What they will do is make every single method its own `interface`. I'm not joking.

5.2 Ever Do Functional Programming in Java?

For this principle, we can't use Ruby, because Ruby has no way to force dependence on anything, and by default all Ruby code complies with this principle (or none of it does, either way, Rubyists can safely ignore this since they totally can't follow it).

We have to use Java, but hey, we're all about polyglot and using the right tool for the right job, and there's no better tool for outlining the complexity of static typing than Java.[3]

In our Java application, we have a database of wrestling matches, and we need access to that database. We'll create a `MatchRepository` class like so:

```
class MatchRepository {
  public Match load(int id) {
    // ...
  }

  public void save(Match match) {
    // ...
  }

  public Set<Match> search(String query) {
    // ...
  }
}
```

We want to write some code that saves a match once it's been completed. That looks like so:

```
public class MatchCompleted {
  public void completeMatch(Match match,
                            Wrestler winner,
                            int time) {
    match.setLength(time / 60);
    match.setWinner(winner);
    (new MatchRepository()).save(match);
  }
}
```

Do you see the horrible design flaw in our code? You might be thinking that `MatchRepository` has a pretty cohesive interface and

---

[3] Yes, I'm aware of Scala, but it's so batshit that you wouldn't be able to learn the complexity since you'd be constantly trying to google what that stupid underscore means. Your eyes would start to glaze over as you suddenly find yourself sitting between someone who desperately wants to use Haskell at work, but can't, and someone who realized that you can't get six figures writing research papers about category theory and had to go work at some fintech startup instead.

so what is the problem? You clearly don't see the deep need to segregate interfaces!

Remember, the principle states that "Clients should not be forced to depend upon interfaces they do not use". Do you see `MatchCompleted` calling `search` or `load`? I don't. How *dare* we force that poor class to depend on those interfaces!

The solution—and I have absolutely seen this done as a direct result of the Interface Segregation Principle—is to create single-method interfaces that the implementation class `implements`.

5.3 Java Loves Interfaces So Much That It Does, In Fact, Marry Them

We first segregate our dirty, dirty `MatchRepository` interfaces.

```
interface MatchLoader {
  public Match load(int id);
}
interface MatchSaver {
  public void save(Match match);
}
interface MatchSearcher {
  public Set<Match> search(String query);
}

class MatchRepository implements
  MatchLoader,
  MatchSaver,
  MatchSearcher {

  // code as before
}
```

Now, `MatchCompleted` can be relieved of the horrors of depending on interfaces it does not use:

```
public class MatchCompleted {
```

```
    private MatchSaver saver;

    public MatchCompleted(MatchSaver saver) {
        this.saver = saver;
    }

    public void completeMatch(Match match,
                              Wrestler winner,
                              int time) {
        match.length = time / 60;
        match.winner = winner;
        saver.save(match);
    }
}
```

If we read the text of Uncle Bob's paper (which, you might notice, only exists online as a Google Doc that someone has thankfully linked to from Wikipedia making it not exactly accessible to someone who wants to really understand it[4]), it *does* talk about cohesion. And if you really think about it, there wasn't a real reason to break up the `MatchRepository` interface since it was pretty cohesive. But that's not what the principle says.

Perhaps it could've said "Classes should ideally depend on cohesive interfaces" or maybe even "Interfaces should be cohesive". It even provides the precious "I" we so desperately need to make the acronym work!

What I'm left with here is just a convoluted re-statement of thinking about cohesion. If developers just focused on *that*, they don't need this strange principle to guide them (especially given that it guides them in the wrong direction). And yes, I have totally seen code like the above. It was so dumb!

---

[4]And if they *did*, how long do we **really** think it's going to be before Google sends Docs off on its incredible journey into the sunset?

6

Dependency Inversion Principle, or: Why 2000s-era Java Code Was Mostly Written in XML

This principle makes me the most angry, because when you dig into it, it's all about perpetuating the lie sold to us by object-orientation, which is that re-use and flexibility are good, desirable, and possible.

Like all good principles, this starts off with a straw man argument so transparent it makes me deeply believe in my heart of hearts that this principle was retconned from how to deal with unit testing in Java.

In his paper[1], Uncle Bob outlines—for once!—the problems the principle he's going to present exists to solve: Bad Design![2]

He outlines three aspects of bad design that the Dependency Inversion Principle will help us avoid.

1. It is hard to change because every change affects too many other parts of the system. (Rigidity)

---

[1] https://web.archive.org/web/20110714224327/http://www.objectmentor.com/resources/articles/dip.pdf

[2] I didn't say they were *detailed* problem statements, just that they existed.

2. When you make a change, unexpected parts of the system break. (Fragility)
3. It is hard to reuse in another application because it cannot be disentangled from the current application. (Immobility)

The first two are real problems. And I believe that a focus on cohesion—and decoupling your implementation when your code becomes incoherent—can address those two problems pretty well. And I also don't think there's any hard and fast rule to magically fix those, otherwise we'd have a programming language that does it. We definitely do not have such a programming language.[3]

Instead, the paper focuses on the third problem which is, let's be honest, entirely invented to make this principle happen. Re-use is such a disingenuous lie, I'm surprised anyone with any real world experience still promotes it as a benefit of object-orientation.

6.1 Objects are All About Re-use. Just ask CORBA... I mean EJB

Here is the code the paper uses to motivate us down the road of inverting our dependencies (I believe it is in C++).

```
void Copy() {
  int c;
  while ((c = ReadKeyboard()) != EOF)
    WritePrinter(c);
}
```

This has some real problems, namely what is `ReadKeyboard` and `WritePrinter`? Where did they come from? I don't think it's fair to develop an object-oriented principle based on some procedural code, so let's convert this to Java and assume some classes exist:

---

[3]This is one of the biggest reasons why Ruby's "programmer happiness" is so damn relevant. If we are going to be struggling with design problems, complexity, and hard to maintain code, anything that gives us a bit of happiness along the way is welcome. Thank you, Matz.

```
public static void copy() {
  Keyboard keyboard = new Keyboard();
  Printer printer  = new Printer();
  int c;
  while ((c = keyboard.read()) != -1) {
    printer.write(c);
  }
}
```

OK, better. Now, the problem with this, according to the paper, is that while `keyboard.read()` and `printer.write()` are "nicely re-usable", `copy` is not.

It's left as an exercise to the reader if `copy` actually *has* to be re-usable. If `copy` is supposed to copy input typed into a keyboard over to a printer, I'd say it's pretty bang-on. I might enterprise the name up a bit and call it `copyFromKeyboardToPrinter`, but only if we really need that disambiguation.

This is the foundation upon which the remaining horrors are laid upon us. You see, the Dependency Inversion Principle states a few things:

- High level modules should not depend upon low level modules. Both should depend upon abstractions.
- Abstractions should not depend upon details. Details should depend upon abstractions.

The takeaway is that since `copy` is a high level module, it should not depend on `keyboard` and `printer` directly (even though it absolutely needs them to do its job).

Read the language carefully here. It doesn't say that high level modules should not depend upon low level modules *only* if there is need to re-purpose the high level module. It doesn't say that at all.

The solution is for `Keyboard` and `Printer` to become abstractions upon which `copy` can safely depend. How are we to know what abstractions to turn them into?

Barring a real use case or actual need, it's unclear. Were we to attempt to create abstractions based on a single data point, we would fail. If Uncle Bob had used the canonical domain of professional wrestling, he would've seen that such a leap of abstraction would be difficult without more than one use case.

But he instead used the strawiest of straw men: I/O. *Of course* we know how to abstract I/O because every programming language's standard library has done so. Thus, it's super obvious how to make this code flexible (setting aside that we didn't necessarily need it to be).

So, to the surprise of no one, we hoist up `Keyboard` to a `Reader` and `Printer` to be a `Writer`. This is how that changes our `copy` method:

```
public static void copy(Reader reader, Writer writer) {
  int c;
  while ((c = reader.read()) != -1) {
    reader.write(c);
  }
}
```

This code no longer works, because we have to now call `copy` with some arguments so that stuff typed at the keyboard gets copied to the printer. We need a main method anyway, so let's make `App`, which holds the `main` method of our program and call the now highly-reusable `copy` method with a `Reader` and `Writer`:

```
public class App {
  public static void main(String []args) {
    Reader keyboard = new Keyboard();
    Writer printer  = new Printer();
    copy(keyboard,printer);
  }
}
```

Uh oh, `App` now depends on the wretched *details* we just took out of copy! `main` isn't re-usable!!!!! We need flexibility people, because we're using *objects*!

6.2 I Will Make FizzBuzz Enterprise Edition Look Like Rails

Since we're not given any bounds or details about when it might be OK for a high level module to depend on details and concretions, we clearly have to keep going. You *did* see how we created dirty actual concrete objects using `new` right? These details have no place in our clean code!

To resolve this design dilemma, we will accept the names of the classes to use on the command line in order to dynamically create them. If some lesser programmer wants to sully their good name with details, they can put the class names in a bash script that invokes our clean Java program.[4]

```
public class App {
  public static void main(String []args) {
    if (args.length < 2) {
      throw new RuntimeException(
          "provide details, oh vile one!");
    }
    Reader reader = (Reader)(Class.forName(args[0]).
        newInstance());
    Writer writer = (Writer)(Class.forName(args[1]).
        newInstance());
    copy(reader,writer);
  }
}
```

This is obviously better, because we now don't have to depend on such measly details as which actual classes to use at runtime. But there's still a problem, right? `main` can only be used to copy things from a reader to a writer. It would be more flexible if it could do other things, too. I mean, it's right there in the name "main". Why do we hold it back from its true calling of doing literally anything?

Clearly, we need to allow our program's first argument to name the class that will do the work while the second argument names the

---

[4]Isn't that where *everyone's* dirty laundry always ends up? On the command line in some bash script. Poor bash.

method to invoke. The remaining arguments will be the names of classes we'll instantiate and pass into that method.

```java
public class App {
  public static void main(String []args) {
    if (args.length < 2) {
      throw new RuntimeException(
          "provide details, oh vile one!");
    }
    Object doer = Class.forName(args[0]).newInstance();
    Method method = null;
    try {
      for (Method m: doer.getClass().getMethods()) {
        if (m.getName().equals(args[1])) {
          method = m;
        }
      }
      if (method == null) {
        throw new RuntimeException("No such method " +
            args[1] + " on " + args[0]);
      }
    }
    catch (SecurityException se) {
      throw new RuntimeException("Sneaky move, sis " + se);
    }
    List<Object> params = new ArrayList<Object>();

    for (int i = 2; i < args.length; i++) {
      params.add(Class.forName(args[i]).newInstance());
    }
    method.invoke(doer, params.toArray());
  }
}
```

Ah, so much better now, right? We have *way* fewer details and our code is much more flexible.[5] And, it's teased out some new

---

[5]Though there is a *huge* risk that the value of 2 will change and we'll forget to update it everywhere we need it. Remember that time they changed the value of "2" in us-east-1 and the entire Internet went down, *except* for Netflix, because Netflix knows how to make abstract constants to use instead of literals? That's why they do all the cool conference talks.

domain concepts we weren't aware of before! This code has *too many responsibilities*! We have the basic need to invoke a method, but we also have code to find that method and convert the args into params.

Let's assume we have tests and Ruthlessly Refactor.

We need a class for finding a method:

```
public class MethodFinder {
  public Method find(Object object, String methodName) {
    Method method = null;
    try {
      for (Method m: object.getClass().getMethod()) {
        if (m.getName().equals(methodName)) {
          method = m;
        }
      }
      if (method == null) {
        throw new RuntimeException("No such method " +
            method);
      }
      return method;
    }
    catch (SecurityException se) {
      throw new RuntimeException("Sneaky move, sis " + se);
    }
  }
}
```

We need one to convert the command line arguments into parameters:

```
public class ArgsToParamsConverter {
  public Object[] convert(String args[], int startIndex) {
    List<Object> params = new ArrayList<Object>();

    for (int i = startIndex; i < args.length; i++) {
      params.add(Class.forName(args[i]).newInstance());
    }
    return params.toArray();
```

    }
}

We now can use those in App. While we're in App, we'll avoid the needless repetition of details like 0 and 1 by using the Oats[6] of object-orientation: constants.

```
public class App {
  private static final INDEX_THAT_HAS_THE_CLASS_NAME = 0;
  private static final INDEX_WITH_THE_METHOD_NAME   = 1;
  private static final INDEX_THAT_STARTS_THE_PARAMS = 2;

  public static void main(String []args) {
    if (args.length < INDEX_THAT_STARTS_THE_PARAMS) {
      throw new RuntimeException(
          "provide details, oh vile one!");
    }
    Object doer = Class.forName(
        args[INDEX_THAT_HAS_THE_CLASS_NAME]).newInstance();
    Method method = new MethodFinder().find(
        doer, args[INDEX_WITH_THE_METHOD_NAME]);
    method.invoke(doer, new ArgsToParamsConverter().convert(
        args,INDEX_WITH_THE_METHOD_NAME));
  }
}
```

Much better, right? You don't think this is an improvement? We did nothing but eliminate pesky details and have code that is high level depend only on abstractions. This is good code right here.[7]

Is this a bad faith argument? Sure, but it points out how unhelpful this principle is. It is unclear about the problem it's trying to solve and then spends most of the paper talking about how to make things flexible. Most software doesn't need to be this flexible!

And all software has *some* module somewhere that has to actually say what objects we are using for what. Right? *RIGHT?*

---

[6]https://en.wikipedia.org/wiki/John_Oates

[7]I'll be honest, if this book doesn't end up being a certain number of pages, I'm coming back to this part and will repeat this until I have enough pages. I will dynamically create a class whose methods' implementations are specified in a .properties file if I have to.

6.3 .java files are for Clean Coders Only

Ever work on a big Spring-based project in Java? In the early 2000s, the way developers avoided the dirty business of creating objects was to *configure* them. You'll note that our App is still woefully coupled to MethodFinder and ArgsToParamsConverter.

Enter dependency injection. We'll assume a class called Context that can read some configuration about what actual objects to use, instantiate them, and then make them available to us:

```
  public static void main(String []args) {
    if (args.length < INDEX_THAT_STARTS_THE_PARAMS) {
      throw new RuntimeException(
          "provide details, oh vile one!");
    }

    Context context = Context.initialize();

    MethodFinder methodFinder =
      (MethodFinder)context.get("MethodFinder");

    ArgsToParamsConverter argsToParamsConverter =
      (ArgsToParamsConverter)context.get("ArgsToParamsConverter");

    Object doer = Class.forName(
        args[INDEX_THAT_HAS_THE_CLASS_NAME]).newInstance();

    Method method = methodFinder.find(
        doer, args[INDEX_WITH_THE_METHOD_NAME]);

    method.invoke(doer, argsToParamsConverter.convert(
        args,INDEX_WITH_THE_METHOD_NAME));
  }
```

What does our configuration file look like? If you guessed "YAML", well, I have some bad news.

```xml
<beans>
  <bean id="MethodFinder" class="MethodFinder" />
  <bean id="ArgsToParamsConverter"
      class="ArgsToParamsConverter" />
</beans>
```

The great thing about this is that when that Principle Engineer we hired[8] sees the horrors of `MethodFinder` and creates `QuickSortBasedMethodIntrospectionLocatorBeanImpl`, we don't have to change the source code to use it![9]

```xml
<beans>
  <bean
    id="MethodFinder"
    class="QuickSortBasedMethodIntrospectionLocatorBeanImpl" />
  <bean
    id="ArgsToParamsConverter"
    class="ArgsToParamsConverter" />
</beans>
```

And they say Ruby is too dynamic.

So how did we get *here*? Well, we followed the principle's advice to avoid depending on details and to instead depend on abstractions. And abstractions we got.

Note that our program does pretty much what it did before. It now has a ton of flexibility which it does not need at all. But if it *did* need it, was *this* the right way to make it flexible? Probably not. But we did make a huge mess and if you have ever done enterprise Java, this is exactly why those codebases are organized the way they are.

What ever happened to the simplest thing that could possibly work? This *can't* be it.

---

[8] Pun absolutely intended.

[9] *HOLY SHIT* we are automatically complying with the Open/Closed Principle because we don't have to change source since who in their right mind would think that XML is actual source code and even if it were, surely it would not be the most critical part of the application and surely if we did do that, we wouldn't require some massive opaque container (not Docker) to execute it, right? Right?

And speaking of agile aphorisms, a lot of them just rub me the wrong way. They feel a lot like SOLID: vague, unhelpful, and slighting demeaning. Let's have a look.

7

Agile's Infantilizing Sloganeering Diminishes Us All

A theme running across my criticism of the SOLID principles is that, as written, they are unclear, vague, and open to potentially dangerous interpretations. It would be better for everyone if the advice they claim to impart was just stated directly.

But SOLID has *nothing* on some other slogans used in the agile community, starting with DRY.

7.1 DRY - Don't Repeat Yourself. Do Not Repeat Yourself. Stop. Repeating. Yourself.

The three words "don't repeat yourself" are pretty terrible advice on their own. It is super normal to repeat yourself when explaining something. People don't necessarily hear you, or they don't understand something the way it's written, or it doesn't make sense the first time. Repeating ourselves helps us explain ourselves. Repetition is also a tool for mastery. Repetition is how we gain experience.

Of course, this isn't exactly what the authors of the Pragmatic Programmer[1] meant when they put this in the book. With a bit more context, DRY states:

---

[1] https://pragprog.com/book/tpp20/the-pragmatic-programmer-20th-anniversary-edition

> Every piece of knowledge must have a single, unambiguous, authoritative representation within a system

Depending on how we interpret this phrase it could mean different things. Does it mean that each piece of knowledge should have only one representation and that that representation should be authoritative? Or does it mean that it doesn't matter how many representations there are, as long as only one of them is considered authoritative?

Most programmers interpret this to mean "don't duplicate anything". The problem with this literal interpretation is that we can't have caching because that duplicates knowledge in our normalized database which would be repeating ourselves (from a certain point of view[2]).

Often, developers will point at code that uses literal values and say "DRY this up", as if the value of 0 is going to change and thus must be abstracted into a constant called ZERO. When you also consider what a horrible detail that is to depend on, you might create this monstrosity:

```
public class CalculateSomeStuff {
  private Integer zero;
  public CalculateSomeStuff(Integer zero) {
    this.zero = zero;
  }
  public int getBest(List<Integer> values) {
    for(Integer i: values) {
      if (i != this.zero) {
        // ...
```

---

[2] Even after he gets struck down by Vader, Obi Wan *still* can't own up to his mistake and cop to his dirty lies. Instead he rationalizes being a total jerk instead of realizing the gravity of the situation and preparing Luke for the task at hand. It's a classic terrible manager tactic. Rather than give Luke a problem to solve ("Defeat the Empire") and the agency to solve it, he dribbles out bits of information to get him to do what he wants the way he wants it. Still, that's better than Holdo who, knowing that Poe is a hot-head take-charge kinda guy, doesn't tell him the freaking plan or that there even *is* a plan. What does Poe do? Take charge! What was Holdo *expecting* to happen? If she had instead made with some leadership and given Poe even a *little* bit of information, we could've been saved from that entire stupid Space Vegas sequence in what was an otherwise pretty awesome Star Wars movie. In conclusion, do not look at Star Wars for leadership lessons.

```
          }
        }
      }
    }

<bean id="zero" class="java.lang.Integer">
  <constructor-arg value="0"/>
</bean>
```

What's really going on with DRY is that you should avoid situations where you have to make the same change multiple times. However, even *this* can lead to problematic outcomes, because our test code often must duplicate some logic of our real code. If we overly "DRY up" our test code, we are left with tests woefully coupled to the code they are testing. This can result in tests that don't fail when the code under test is broken.

Instead of yelling "DRY" in a code review, we should be talking about the cost of a particular duplication and being clear what it is. For example, when thinking about data in a database, there *should* be a single *authoritative* representation of a fact in the system, but there can be (and often must be) several non-authoritative representations such as caches. That is duplication. That is a form of "repeating yourself", but it is necessary.

7.2 KISS - I'm not Stupid, and Neither Are You

"KISS" is often used when code is complex. KISS stands for Keep It Simple Stupid. You know what? I'm not stupid. I'm just not. And neither are you. I don't need to be insulted in order to discuss code. Maybe you think it should be "Keep It Simple Silly", but I don't think it's silly to overcomplicate code. Everyone does it. It is normal.

KISS is trying to tell us a good thing: keep your solutions simple[3]. And we often need to be reminded of this when thinking through solutions or writing code. That said, calling me stupid is not the best way to do that.

---
[3]Which would be "KYSS", which is ironically a much better metal band name than "KISS".

I also don't think it's too hard to just say "Keep it simple" or "don't build software to solve problems you don't have" or "build for only what you need". Sure, they don't result in nice English acronyms that we can scream at junior developers who are just trying their best, but if we just said directly what we mean and explain why... wouldn't that be better than calling everyone stupid?

7.3 YAGNI - You Aren't Gonna Need It (except when you are)

Ron Jeffries (who coined the phrase), you don't know what I **need**. And if you *did* know what I need, why don't you just tell me and stop shaming me while I try to wrestle with a challenging software problem?

Like KISS, YAGNI's heart is in the right place. It says to not build things you don't need and to not solve problems you don't have. This is the same lesson taught to us by KISS. Talk about not repeating yourself.

YAGNI is pernicious because the words as written can't be properly understood without a ton of context. Most developers lack this context. They use YAGNI to excuse a lack of tests, lack of writing log statements, not improving variable names when writing code, or simply writing messy code.

As with KISS, it is far more useful to talk plainly about the issue, which is if you build software to meet needs you don't have, that software will have a carrying cost that might make it harder to add features or fix bugs later, and it is unlikely to save time in the future. Thus, building for things you don't know you need is not a good tradeoff.

7.4 The Simplest Thing That Could Possibly Work Would Be Actually Working Software

I've had a lot of jobs as a programmer over my 20+ years of experience, and in all of those jobs, it was expected that I make—or try to make—software that *actually did* work. If I had turned in code and said "it's possible that this could work"... that would've been a problem.

The specific words of this phrase lead us astray. We should be trying to write software that actually does work, and setting that part of this aside, we are left with "simple", and thus we have a *third* agile maxim telling us to keep our code simple and to not solve problems we don't have. Perhaps if the progenitors of XP had just said this directly, we wouldn't have wound ourselves around *three* silly acronyms that don't provide real guidance.

7.5 No Big Design Up Front So Why Aren't You Coding Right Now? Start Coding. Now. Just Type "v" "i" "m"...

"No Big Design Up Front" or "No BDUF" is almost always interpreted as "don't think, code!" I know that's not what was meant, but if you remove or misinterpret what "Big" means, you get very bad advice. The number of problems I have seen developers create (myself included) by not just *taking a moment to think* before coding is large.

The thing is, if you know what BDUF means, you don't need this slogan, and if you *don't* know what it means, it will provide absolutely no help. "No BDUF" means that you don't do a massive detailed design of everything before you start. It *does not* mean that you don't do *any* design.

It's worth considering that because of the very agile manifesto than gave rise to these aphorisms, the chance of your average developer actually encountering a waterfall project with a truly Big Design is pretty low. Most developers don't really know a Big Design when they see one so if you ask them to write a one-pager before they get started on a thorny feature, they balk: "No BDUF".

The other effect this has is to shame people who can't simply just start coding, but need to sketch things out, think them through, or make a rough plan first. And you throw pair programming into the mix and now you have perfectly capable developers thinking they are stupid because someone said "NO BDUF BRUH DO YOU EVEN CODE?"

7.6 User Stories Paint a Picture of Fairy Tales and Form Validations

What is a "story"? According to the dictionary, it is:

> an account of imaginary or real people and events told for entertainment.

That does not sound like the basis for breaking down the requirements of a software system to me. It only gets stranger when we look into the definition of "user story".

The coiner of the phrase defines it as a "promise for a conversation". Is that supposed to be a joke? I guess we put these stories in the parking lot next to all the chores, right?

The way most people treat user stories is that they are specific requirements for how the software should work, written from the user's perspective. For example, "As a wrestling booker, I want to make the main event of Monday Night Raw a cage match".

Being user-focused is a good thing and coercing requirements to be written from a user's perspective makes sense. But we are not children attending grade school who must be coddled into doing our jobs, nor are the people asking us to write software. In fact, we are all adults[4] and professionals.[5]

I'm actually not sure why we can't just say "user requirements". The barest interpretation of this phrase is "stuff that the user

---

[4] It is worth remembering that there are a *lot* of people running companies who do not know how software or technology works and also do not trust professionals by default, so they do, in fact, need to be treated like babies in order to allow software to be developed. In these cases, infantile words and cute aphorisms can absolutely help, but I think we do ourselves a disservice by saying this is how it has to be or is the best way to describe this stuff. I think the world would be a better place if people running technology companies understood how software worked. Kindergarten language doesn't get us there.

[5] That being said, we have to also keep in mind that a lot of programmers, if left unattended, will create massive complexity and problems writing software because writing software is a helluva lot of fun. Sometimes it's just kinda boring to build out a simple web form based on server-rendered views, so tools to keep the developers focused are good, too. But I still think it would be better (and maybe even more effective) if we just said what we meant directly and clearly instead of dressing it up in childish slogans.

requires of the software", and that *is* what we are trying to suss out, right?

A secondary goal of user stories is to encourage developers to break down complex requirements into small, shippable units that can be demonstrated for the purpose of getting feedback. The reality of software is that users don't exactly know what they want until they have something to react to. So the way user stories are defined encourages us to get things in front of users early and often. This is good.

But why must we misuse language and be overly cute to dance around the point? Is it *really* so hard to explain it directly? "Let's break this feature down into small, shippable chunks we can demonstrate because then we can get feedback quickly about how well we're doing."

If you've been on an agile project, you have no doubt wasted a sizeable chunk of your life debating what is a "story" and what is a "task" and what is a "chore" and on and on. This is telling you that the language you've chosen to adopt is failing you.

Would it not be simpler to call each and every thing a developer does a "task"? A "task" is "a piece of work to be done". Simple, right? Aren't we all about simple?

And how do we figure out the tasks? We write down what the requirements are in plain language and try to ship some of that. Calling those "user stories" and fitting them to a template isn't exactly helping. If the only way we know to be user-focused is some template, then I'm sorry, but we're in more serious trouble and JIRA can't help.

We really do have to think it through and no cutesy language is going to keep us from having to do that. No templates will make us magically good at it when we otherwise aren't. We have to do it and do it and do it. We have to keep at it to become experienced. We have to repeat ourselves, right?

8

Well, *Now* What Do We Do?

Researching and writing this has led me to a single conclusion: ignore SOLID. You'll be fine. Your biggest problem will be steering developers away from it when they join your team.[1]

This journey *has* given me some confidence in how to discuss *actual* design problems with software as well as the ability to quickly stop talking about SOLID and talk about real code and real problems. I hope it's helped you as well.

8.1 Some Solid Advice

The best lessons I've learned weren't rules, principles, or axioms, but were frameworks for how to think about problems. To this end, here is what this journey through SOLID has taught me about how to think about the problems of software development.

- If you can't articulate the problem, the solution will become a second problem.
- Build software for what you need, but be clear about what "need" means.
- Software that's easy to change isn't flexible or configurable, it's simple and well-tested.
- Always ask "Why?" And keep asking until you get an answer.

---

[1]Which, let's be honest, is only really the Single Responsibility Principle, since no one understands O, L, and I, and D only makes sense for Java projects and if I have to work on another Java project, I will pull my hair out and go sell Brutalist bird houses from an Etsy store instead.

8.2 Some Words of Warning

Developers in positions of power who can't articulate the problem being solved *really* hate being asked to do so. Some developers just cannot handle being asked to explain themselves. You could make your life miserable by getting on the bad side of these people. Be careful.

But if you feel safe being bold enough to question authority, you will find solidarity. Every time you ask some senior engineer why they keep going on and on about immutability, there are five other engineers with the same question and you all deserve an answer.

8.3 Not Convinced?

First, there are no refunds. Second, I invite you to create a blog post or even a book in rebuttal to this. It's easier to make a book than you think!

In fact, I would *love* to read something medium or long form in rebuttal to this or in defense of SOLID. I would *not* like to read your hot take in 280 characters or fewer (and I'm not *that* interested in going to Hacker News, either).

All you have to do is learn LaTeX.

9

Colophon or: How To Make Your Own e-Book!

You want your book to look great, right? You want it to be *at least* as awesome as this one and that means learning a bit of LaTeX.[1]

But, you can get a lot of the way there by doing what I did, which is to write the thing in Markdown[2], then use Pandoc[3] to turn it into a PDF or EPUB.

If you are using a computer, however, this is incredibly difficult because installing LaTeX is not for the faint of heart. You should do what I did and install it in a Docker[4] container, then create a series of shell scripts and makefiles.

This will get you the default LaTeX styling. If you've ever read a *real* computer science paper (one from a journal, not one written by an agile thought leader), you will recognize the tell-tale wide margins and the you'll-know-it-when-you-see-it Computer Modern typeface. And we will all know you used the defaults, which is almost as shameful as writing code that depends on details!

To help you, I will share my secret. That secret is the Memoir document class[5], which allows customizing things. I arranged for the body text to be set in Utopia[6] with chapter titles set in ITC

---

[1] Some people think if you can learn Webpack, you can learn anything. They have not heard of Kubernetes. Those that have, think if you can learn Kubernetes, you can learn anything. *They* have not heard of LaTeX.
[2] https://daringfireball.net/projects/markdown/
[3] https://pandoc.org
[4] https://www.docker.com
[5] https://ctan.org/pkg/memoir
[6] http://en.wikipedia.org/wiki/Utopia_(typeface)

Avant Garde Gothic[7]. The code listings use Inconsolata[8] and the dimensions of the pages and text block are related to the golden ratio.[9]

You don't have to do any of that, but be warned: arguments made in Arial do not hold.

---

[7]http://en.wikipedia.org/wiki/ITC_Avant_Garde
[8]http://en.wikipedia.org/wiki/Inconsolata
[9]The EPUB and Kindle versions probably look like crap and I'm sorry, but this is what happens when the e-reader market is dominated by a company that makes most of its money selling overpriced servers that you configure with JSON.

Milton Keynes UK
Ingram Content Group UK Ltd.
UKHW021603070524
442346UK00039B/639